Popular PROVERBS

SONIA MEHTA

PUFFIN BOOKS
An imprint of Penguin Random House

PUFFIN BOOKS

USA | Canada | UK | Ireland | Australia
New Zealand | India | South Africa | China | Singapore

Puffin Books is part of the Penguin Random House group of companies whose addresses can be found at global.penguinrandomhouse.com

Published by Penguin Random House India Pvt. Ltd
4th Floor, Capital Tower 1, MG Road,
Gurugram 122 002, Haryana, India

Penguin Random House India

First published in Puffin Books by Penguin Random House India 2018

10 9 8 7 6 5 4 3 2

ISBN 9780143444893

Design and layout by Quadrum Solutions Pvt. Ltd

Printed at Repro India Limited

www.penguin.co.in

Dear MOMS and DADS

Over the years, I have discovered that the smartest, most confident kids, are those who have great language and communication skills. They are able to get their thoughts and ideas across in the most effective way, and this helps build their confidence.

And one of the best ways to help them develop these skills, is to give them a strong foundation. We recognize that English is a language that will remain important to them in their future lives—both professional and personal. Which is why, in the **Fun with English** series of books, we have focussed on bringing alive those aspects of the language that will add flair to children's communication when they speak or write.

English is a language that has many subtle nuances. The simplest sentence can be brought alive with an appropriate idiom, a well-chosen figure of speech or a colourful proverb. The correct use of punctuation and phonic sounds adds dramatically to the written or spoken word. By focussing creatively on all these, the **Fun with English** series aims to help kids get comfortable with some of the more confusing aspects of the language in a manner that is exciting and challenging.

I've enjoyed writing these books and I've re-discovered the joy of English as I did. I hope you enjoy these books with your children too.

SONIA MEHTA

Hello KIDS

You probably already know what a proverb is. Over hundreds of years, wise folk have found the perfect words to tell us important things we need to remember.

For example,

AN APPLE A DAY, KEEPS THE DOCTOR AWAY.

What this means is that when you eat food that is good for you (like apples), you will keep yourself healthy and you won't need to see a doctor at all.

Proverbs are short, colourful sayings that usually communicate advice or something that is generally true. There are many, many proverbs in English that make the message colourful and memorable too! You will discover many new proverbs as you work through the activities in this book. If you get stuck at any point, ask a grown-up for help or use a dictionary or the Internet.

I do hope you enjoy this book as much as I have enjoyed writing it. I'd love to hear from you. So do write to me and let me know if you liked this book.

Lots of love,

SONIA AUNTY

PS: Do e-mail me if you have anything you'd like to say about this book.

sonia.mehta@quadrumltd.com

Before You Begin

Here is a list of proverbs and their meanings. There are many more proverbs you will discover as you complete the activities in this book. Enjoy!

1. A rolling stone gathers no moss.
   A person who keeps moving from place to place will not gain anything.
2. Actions speak louder than words.
   What someone does has a greater impact than what they just say they will do.
3. An eye for an eye and a tooth for a tooth.
   To punish someone for harming a person by having the same thing done to them.
4. Ask no questions and hear no lies.
   Don't ask a question if you don't want to be lied to.
5. Beggars cannot be choosers.
   Someone who doesn't have a choice can't afford to be picky.
6. Birds of a feather flock together.
   People who are similar will naturally want to be around each other.
7. Charity begins at home.
   First do good in your neighbourhood or community, then the rest of the world.
8. Don't put the cart before the horse.
   Do things in the right order.
9. Blood is thicker than water.
   Family is more important than other relationships.
10. Don't bite the hand that feeds you.
    Don't hurt someone who is supporting you.
11. Better late than never.
    It's better to do something important late than never do it at all.
12. Don't count your chickens before they are hatched.
    Don't collect your reward before you have seen the results.
13. Empty vessels make the most noise.
    People with the least ability talk the most.
14. A rising tide lifts all boats.
    A good outcome benefits everyone.
15. As you make your bed, so you must lie on it.
    You get what you deserve.
16. It's no use locking the stable door after the horse has bolted.
    It's no use taking precautions after the damage has been done.
17. Don't put all your eggs in one basket.
    Don't rely on just one thing to give you what you want.
18. All work and no play makes Jack a dull boy.
    Being too focused on work and forgetting to have fun makes you boring.

The Right Choice

Old Mr Dogsbody has some advice to give us all. Can you choose the right words to complete the proverbs below?

1. You can't teach an old ____________ new tricks.
(It means that it's difficult to teach older people a new way of doing things.)

caterpillar   alligator   dog

2. Don't bite the ____________ that feeds you.
(It means we must not hurt those who help or support us.)

hand   arm   thumb

3. There are plenty of ____________ in the sea.
(It means there are many opportunities for everyone.)

plastic bottles   fish   octopuses

4. The early bird gets the ____________.
(It means if you make an early start, you will be more likely to succeed.)

butterfly   worm   cockroach

5. From the frying pan, into the ____________.
(It means that you're going from a bad situation right into another, that's even worse.)

swimming pool   fire   jacuzzi

Crazy Crossword

Can you solve this crossword using the clues below?

DOWN

1. A ________ dog seldom bites. (Someone who makes a lot of threats isn't always harmful.)
2. A bad ________ blames his tools. (People who are not good at their job blame everything but themselves.)
6. A drowning man will clutch a ________. (A desperate person will take any kind of help.)

ACROSS

3. A ________ penny always turns up. (Someone who is nasty or unpleasant always shows up even if you don't want them to.)
4. To upset the ________ cart. (To spoil something for everyone.)
5. All that ________ is not gold. (Everything that looks attractive on the surface isn't necessarily good.)
7. Every ________ has his day. (Every person, however simple, has a moment that makes them special.)
8. A ________ never changes its spots. (A person can never change the most basic thing about themselves.)

Match Them Right . . .

Mrs Matchmaker wants to match these phrases to make proverbs. Can you help her match the right and left columns?

a rolling stone •	• a tooth for a tooth
actions speak •	• and hear no lies
an eye for an eye and •	• flock together
ask no questions •	• louder than words
beggars cannot be •	• at home
birds of a feather •	• gathers no moss
charity begins •	• choosers

. . . Write Them Out

And now write down the proverbs you made on the previous page below their meanings.

1. Someone who wanders around without purpose cannot become stable and successful.

   ____

2. What you do means much more than just what you say.

   ____

3. Punishing someone by taking from them what they took from you.

   ____

4. Don't ask me anything because I can't tell you the truth.

   ____

5. When there are so few options, you can't be picky.

   ____

6. People who are alike usually stick together.

   ____

7. Do something for your own community or neighbourhood before helping others.

   ____

Tick Tock

Mr Jumbleweed is always getting his proverbs mixed up. Can you help him out by ticking (✓) the right word so he gets his proverbs right? Then write down the meanings of the proverbs.

1. A bird/turtle/snake in the hand is worth two in the bush.

   ____

   ____

2. A bullet/see-saw/chain is only as strong as its weakest link.

   ____

   ____

3. A friend in need is a enemy/colleague/friend indeed.

   ____

   ____

4. A penny saved is a penny/coin/pig earned.

   ____

   ____

5. A stitch in time saves nine/ten/eleven.

   ____

   ____

Juggle Muggle

Joey Juggler has got all his balls in the air. Can you sort them for him by colouring both the proverb and the meaning using the same colour?

- Better to do something later rather than not do it at all.
- Do things in the right order.
- Families are closer than friends.
- Don't be ungrateful.
- Don't put the cart before the horse.
- First learn the basics. Then do the harder things.
- Blood is thicker than water.
- Don't bite the hand that feeds you.
- Don't try to run before you can walk.
- Better late than never.
- Don't collect your reward before you have seen the results.
- Don't count your chickens before they are hatched.

Going Blank

Mr Furry loves animals. He loves proverbs that feature animals. But even he can't remember which animal goes with which proverb. Can you help him? Choose the right animal to complete these proverbs.

dog	camel	lion	mice	hippopotamus
horses	bird	cat	fleas	bugs
	cockroaches		flies	

1. A closed mouth catches no ____________.
   (When people don't chatter on unnecessarily, they are less likely to say something wrong.)
2. If wishes were ____________, beggars would ride.
   (If wishes could easily come true, then even the poorest would be rich and get what they want.)
3. It's the early ____________ that catches the worm.
   (When you begin early, you are more likely to succeed.)
4. When the cat's away the ____________ will play.
   (When there is no one to supervise, people will get up to mischief.)
5. If you lie down with dogs, you will get up with ____________.
   (If you keep bad company, you will get bad habits.)

Lost Words

Careless Carrie has misplaced some words. Can you help find them? They're hidden in the word grid.

A	S	C	D	R	F	T	H	Y	N
F	L	E	M	O	N	A	D	E	H
Q	W	E	R	T	Y	U	I	O	C
C	A	S	T	L	E	S	D	F	G
Z	S	E	R	D	C	V	F	T	Y
G	B	N	H	U	H	E	A	R	T
Z	A	W	S	X	C	D	E	R	F
B	R	I	D	G	E	S	A	S	D
A	S	E	D	R	F	T	G	H	Y
A	S	W	C	A	N	D	L	E	V
D	P	I	C	T	U	R	E	D	S

1. If life gives you lemons, make ______________.
(Make the best of what you get.)

2. A ______________ is worth a thousand words.
(An image can make more of an impression than many words to describe the same thing.)

3. Absence makes the ______________ grow fonder.
(When you are apart from someone, you feel more strongly about them.)

4. An Englishman's home is his ______________.
(A person's home is a safe place where they can do what they want.)

5. Better to light a ______________ than curse the darkness.
(Take action instead of merely complaining.)

Crack the Code

Detective Dan needs to crack this code to read the secret message below. Can you help him out? Here is a hint: when you do something in a hurry, you will probably do it wrong, and your effort will be in vain.

4 = E   1 = H   8 = W   2 = A   6 = S
3 = T   5 = M   7 = K

1	2	6	3	4

5	2	7	4	6

8	2	6	3	4

Egg-Stra-Ordinary

Dizzy Dolly has realized that in order to achieve something, sometimes bad things happen. But to understand that, she needs to solve this puzzle. Can you help her solve it and complete the proverb?

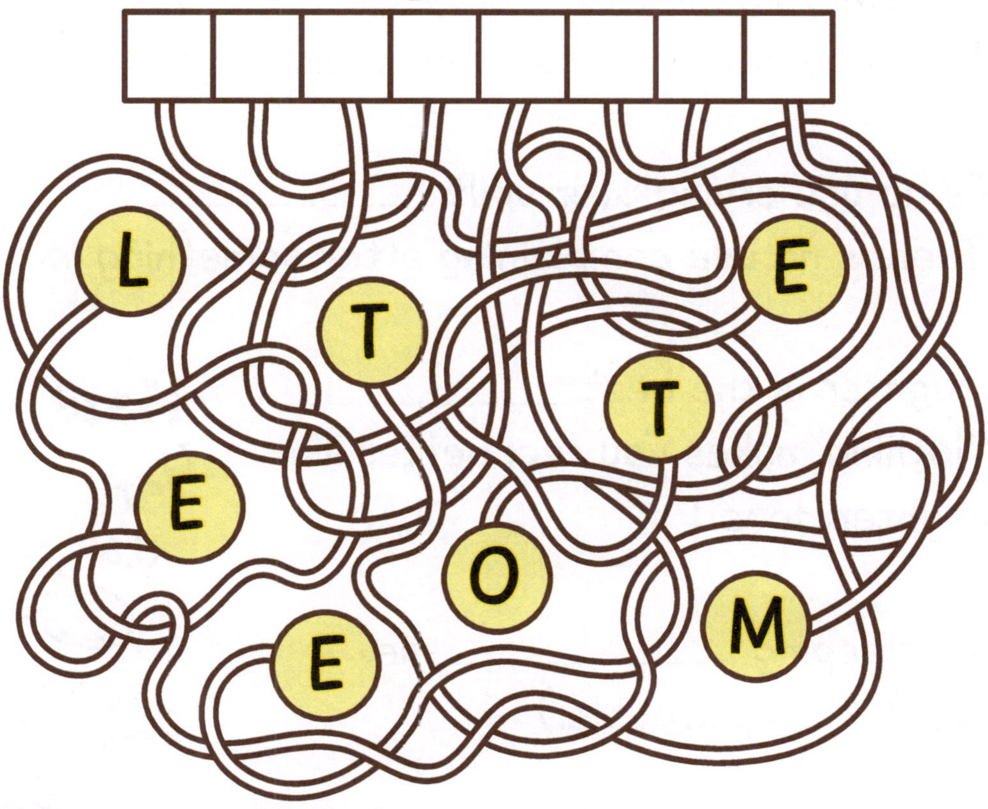

You can't make an ________________ without breaking eggs.

Picture Search

Messy Millie has such a messy room. These proverbs are all over the place. Can you complete them by finding the missing word in Messy Millie's room?

1. Half a loaf is better than no ____________.
   (Something is better than nothing.)

2. Into every life, a little ____________ must fall.
   (Everyone has some bad luck sometimes.)

3. It's no use crying over spilt ____________.
   (There's no use complaining after something is over.)

4. Laughter is the best ____________.
   (Nothing makes you feel better like laughter does.)

5. Let sleeping ____________ lie.
   (Don't stir up trouble.)

6. Never judge a ____________ by its cover.
   (Things are not always the way they look.)

book
milk
bread
dogs
rain
medicine

Crazy Crossword

Clever Carol loves doing crosswords. But she seems to be stuck. Can you help her out?

DOWN

1. Empty ________ make the most noise.
2. A rising tide lifts all ________.
5. Every cloud has a ________ lining.
7. As you make your ________, so you must lie upon it.

ACROSS

3. It's no use locking the stable door after the ______ has bolted.
4. Don't put all your ________ in one basket.
6. All work and no ________ makes Jack a dull boy.
7. Don't cross the ________ till you come to it.

The Proverb Bag

Bertha is trying to keep her bags together. Help her along by matching the proverb to its meaning. Colour both the proverb and its meaning using the same colour.

Decoded

Stu the spy is trying to decode this message. Can you help him crack it? It means that someone who looks simple might actually be very complicated.

1 = S	2 = T	3 = I	4 = L	5 = W	6 = A
7 = E	8 = R	9 = U	10 = N	11 = D	12 = P

1 2 3 4 4

5 6 2 7 8 1

8 9 10

11 7 7 12

Jumbledore

Jumbledore has mixed up his words as usual. Can you help by unscrambling them?

1. All is fair in ________ EOVL and war.
   (In love and in battle, everything is considered fair.)

2. Silly Sally cut off her ________ ESON to spite her face.
   (Silly Sally did something that harmed her.)

3. Early to bed, early to rise, makes you healthy, wealthy and ________ SWIE.
   (Those who lead a disciplined life will achieve success.)

4. Empty vessels make the most ________ IOSEN.
   (Those who have nothing sensible to say are the ones who talk the most.)

5. Make hay while the ________ NSU shines.
   (Make the most of opportunity when it comes.)

Pathfinder

Can you find the proverb hidden in the maze? Colour the blocks and spot the proverb that means do something right away rather than postponing it.

Start

never	always	sometimes	bed	bear
put	off	fish	computer	screen
hangar	until	tomorrow	fan	house
ship	hour	what	you	mist
ocean	moment	word	can	do
finger	sentence	bird	angry	today

Finish

Tick-Tack-Toe

Mr Tricky Tick needs to tick the right answer. Go on. Help him out by ticking (✓) the right word so that the proverb makes sense.

1. Rain/Thunder/Lightning never strikes twice in the same place. (Misfortune doesn't come twice to someone.)
2. People who live in glass/steel/wooden houses shouldn't throw stones. (Those who have something to hide should not accuse other people.)
3. Oil/Perfume/Milk and water don't mix. (People who are not alike often don't get along.)
4. Like cousin/father/grandfather, like son. (Children are like their parents.)
5. Better an empty purse, than an empty neck/toe/head. (It's better to have no money than have no sense.)

Giddy Grid

Giddy Greta is spinning around in circles trying to find the words in the grid so she can complete the proverbs. Can you help her out?

1. Strike while the ____________ is hot
(Make the most of an opportunity.)

2. The hand that rocks the ____________ rules the world.
(Mothers can make their children strong and successful.)

3. There's no ____________ without fire.
(There's always some truth behind a rumour or incident.)

4. Two is company, but three's a ____________.
(Two people can talk better together than three.)

5. See no evil, hear no ____________, speak no evil.
(Don't create trouble and mind your own business.)

6 All's well that ends ____________. (If the end result is good, whatever happened before that doesn't count.)

7 A fool and his ____________ are soon parted. (A foolish person is easily duped by someone.)

8 Fortune favours the ____________. (Courageous will be rewarded.)

A	I	S	D	F	G	H
C	R	N	L	S	K	J
Z	O	C	V	M	B	N
Y	N	C	R	O	W	D
U	T	W	Q	K	C	M
E	V	I	L	E	X	Z
J	R	E	A	N	V	B
B	C	R	A	D	L	E
B	M	O	N	E	Y	A
C	D	B	R	A	V	E
W	E	L	L	E	F	G

Hard Work

Hardworking Harry has a big task. He has to pack a room full of boxes. He starts with one because he believes that getting started even in a small way, is the first step. He wants to share his advice. Can you solve the puzzle and help him complete his message?

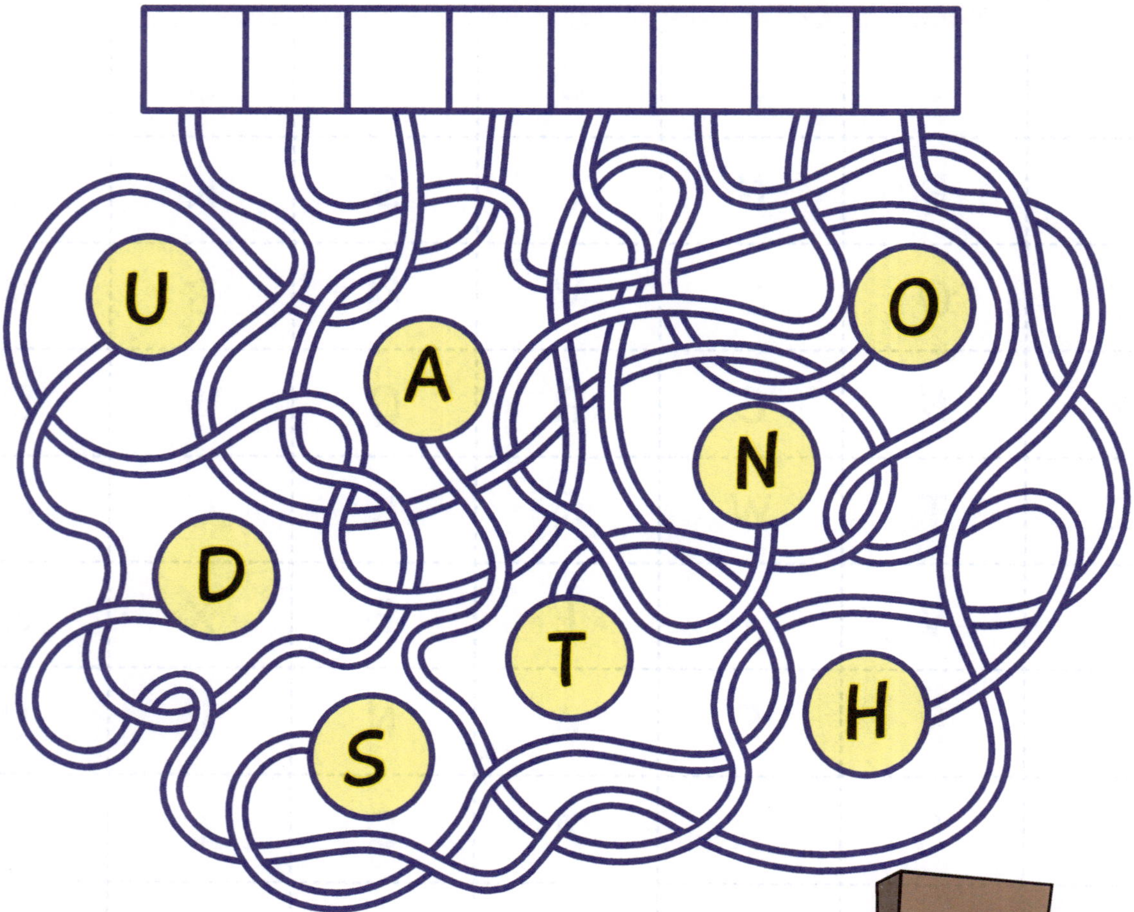

A journey of a ____________ miles
begins with a single step.

Blank It Out

Forgetful Felix is always giving advice. But he keeps forgetting key words. Can you help him by filling in the blanks using words from the box?

castle	house	bush	grass	beauty
coward	boats	heart	lung	stomach

1. A ____________ divided against itself cannot stand.
(When there are arguments within a family, it will never stay strong and be together.)

2. ____________ is in the eye of the beholder.
(If you think something is lovely, then it is.)

3. Don't let the ____________ grow under your feet.
(Don't keep doing the same thing for too long, or you will not succeed.)

4. A rising tide lifts all ____________.
(A good outcome benefits everyone.)

5. Home is where the ____________ is.
(The place you love is your true home.)

Messy Metre

The Messy family has gone on a picnic, but what a mess they've left behind! Can you find the words hidden in the mess to complete the proverbs? Maybe the Messy family could learn a thing or two.

1. A new ________________ sweeps clean.
   (Someone with new ideas can change things for the better.)

2. ________________ is next to godliness.
   (Being clean is very important.)

3. Penny-wise and ________________ foolish.
   (To look after the small things, but make mistakes in the bigger things.)

4. There's no such thing as a free ________________.
   (Everything has a price.)

5. Never let the ________________ go down on your anger.
   (Never go to bed without dealing with your feelings.)

6. The ________________ never falls far from the tree.
   (Children often grow up to be like their parents.)

pound
broom
lunch
apple
sun
cleanliness

Crazy Crossword

Clever Cora knows all the answers. But she's stuck this time. Can you solve this crossword using the words from the box?

gift	Italy	yes	will	hut	home
speared	cured	spice	sight	Rome	London

DOWN

1 Never look a __________ horse in the mouth.
(Never be nasty to a person who is giving you something.)

3 Variety is the __________ of life.
(Experiencing different things is what makes life interesting.)

4 There's no place like __________.
(The best place to be is in your own house.)

5 What can't be __________ must be endured.
(If you cannot change something, you must accept it.)

ACROSS

2 Where there is a __________, there is a way.
(If you really want to do something, you will find a way.)

3 Out of __________, out of mind.
(When something is not in front of you, you can easily forget it.)

6 __________ wasn't built in a day.
(It takes time to achieve something great.)

Jumbled Up Proverbs

Master Muddle mixed up his words. Can you unscramble them and get these proverbs right?

1. Too many OKOSC ________ spoil the broth
   (When too many people get involved in something they make a mess of it.)

2. Don't judge a book by its RCVOE ________.
   (Everything is not what it seems like from the outside.)

3. You can't have your AKEC ________ and eat it too.
   (You can't get everything.)

4. When in Rome, do as the ORANMS ________ do.
   (When you go to someone's house, or city, try and behave like them.)

5. Don't cross the DRIBEG ________ until you come to it.
   (There's no point worrying about something in advance.)

Merry Maze

Joey Juggler is lost. He needs to find his way out of this maze by guessing the proverb that means something that is good for one person may be very bad for another person.

Start

one	heaven	box	run
man's	meat	balloon	line
pencil	is	another	man's
wall	phone	paint	poison

Finish

Ticked Off

Picky Pam has to make a choice. She needs to choose the right word so that the proverb makes sense.

1. ____________ comes but once a year.
   (Opportunity comes only once in a while.)
   picnics sandwiches Christmas

2. Don't leave your manners on the ____________.
   (Remember your good manners wherever you go.)
   doorstep bathroom kitchen

3. Fight fire with ____________.
   (Fight back in the same way that someone is fighting you.)
   water milk fire

4. Go the extra ____________.
   (Do something more than what is expected of you.)
   walk kilometre mile

5. It takes a thief to catch a ________.
   (Only a dishonest person will know what another dishonest person can do.)
   joker athlete thief

Match Them Right . . .

Jolly the Jigsaw Man is really good at matching things. But he can't seem to match these phrases to complete the proverbs. Can you help him out?

ignorance •	• your bread is buttered
it takes all sorts •	• is right
know which side •	• no gain
might •	• is bliss
no pain, •	• to make a world

... Write Them Out

And now write the proverbs you made on the previous page below their meanings.

1. Only the ignorant can be entirely carefree.

2. The world is full of different types of people.

3. To know what is best for you.

4. The strongest people are those who get their way.

5. You can't achieve success without effort.

Gridlocked

Everything in Proverb Ville has come to a standstill because some words have gone missing. Can you find the missing words in the grid and get things moving again in Proverb Ville?

Q	W	E	R	T	Y	U	I
U	A	N	G	E	L	S	E
A	S	D	F	G	H	M	D
Z	X	C	V	B	N	A	C
H	A	N	D	S	T	L	W
Q	E	F	A	L	L	L	E
Z	S	X	D	S	H	O	E

1. Many ________ make light work. (When many people come together, the work becomes easy to do.)
2. Pride goes before a ________. (When someone is too proud, they suffer a comedown.)
3. If the ________ fits, wear it. (Accept something if it applies to you.)
4. Fools rush in where ________ fear to tread. (Silly people do things that wiser people stay away from.)
5. Good things come in ________ packages. (The best things in life are often not big.)

Proverb Maze

Mixed-up Margie is lost. Can you help her find her way through the maze by colouring the blocks that make up the proverb that means good health is more important than money.

Start

better	cart	rush	rose	beggar
to	be	lotus	park	sad
mother	poor	help	themselves	plush
cousin	and	seek	fast	enough
wealthy	healthy	than	be	happy
moneyed	funny	be	rosy	and
plenty	strong	rich	and	sick

Finish

Jumble Tumble

Oops! Miss Bumble the teacher has jumbled up the words in the proverbs she is teaching her class. Can you help her sort them out?

1. A ____________ OSUEH is not a home.
(Just four walls don't make a home. You need to have people too!)

2. All good things must come to an ________ NDE.
(Even happy times come to an end at some point.)

3. As you ________ WSO, so shall you reap.
(You will have to bear the results of your actions.)

4. Cut your ________ TCAO to suit your cloth.
(You must adapt yourself to suit your circumstances.)

5. First come ________ ITRSIF served.
(Those who come first, will get the first chance.)

Hidden Words

Here are some proverbs to do with clothes. Can you find the missing word in the proverb using the clues?

Don't wash your dirty ________________ in public

(Don't talk about your private problems in front of the whole world.)

Trader Tom is a smart businessman. Here's a proverb that he believes in.

Don't kill the goose that lays the ______________ eggs.

(Don't destroy something that gives you something useful.)

Cityscape

What a busy city! There are eight words hidden in the city to complete the proverbs. Can you find them all?

1. ________________ makes perfect.

   (When you do something again and again, you become good at it.)

2. Better safe than ________________.

   (It's better to be careful from the beginning than regret something later.)

3. ________________ never prosper.

   (People who lie will never succeed.)

4. The pen is mightier than the ________________.

   (You can make more of a difference by writing about something than by fighting about it.)

5. Necessity is the ________________ of invention.

   (When you are totally stuck, new ideas come to your mind.)

6. ________________ do not make a man.

   (The way a man dresses does not make him a better person.)

horse
clothes
sword
cheats
mother
practice

Amazing Maze

Naughty Nona loves to confuse people. She has hidden a proverb in this maze that means you must never postpone what you have to do, but do it right away.

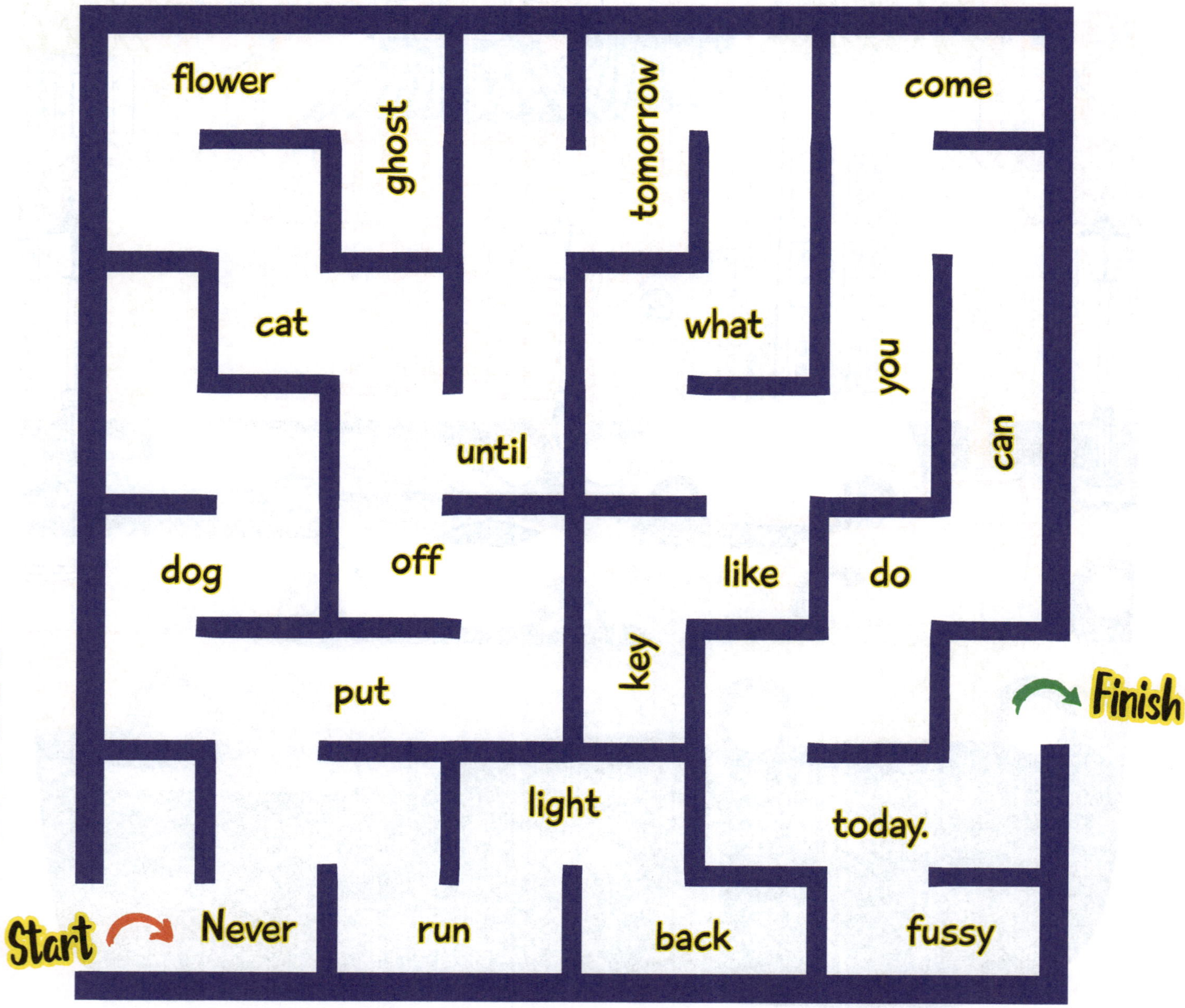

Mixed Up

Mixed-up Mary has got her proverbs all mixed up as usual.
Can you rearrange the words so that the proverbs make sense?

1. trades master all of Jack of none

   ____

   (When you try many things, you become an expert in nothing.)

2. rod spoil the spare and child the

   ____

   (Let a child have his way without ever punishing him, and you can be sure that you will spoil the child.)

3. leap look you before

   ____

   (Be careful before you take any step.)

4. pay cook better than doctor the the

   ____

   (It's better to eat healthy rather than fall sick and have to call the doctor.)

5. sorrow joy sleep the bed same and in

   ____

   (Life is a mix of happiness and sadness.)

Maze-O-Clock

Lost Lola is lost in a maze. She needs to find the words of the proverb that means you must keep all your options open and not bank on just one thing. Can you help her by colouring the boxes and finding a way through the maze?

Start

don't	tin	sandwich	pen	door	table
ever	put	all	table	paper	cotton
plant	grass	your	eggs	in	pain
lawn	green	elephant	book	one	basket

Finish

Lazy Luke

Lazy Luke is always postponing things. His mother tells him that it's not good to do that because he will never find the right day to do something. But she isn't getting the proverb right. Will you help her by solving the puzzle and filling in the blank?

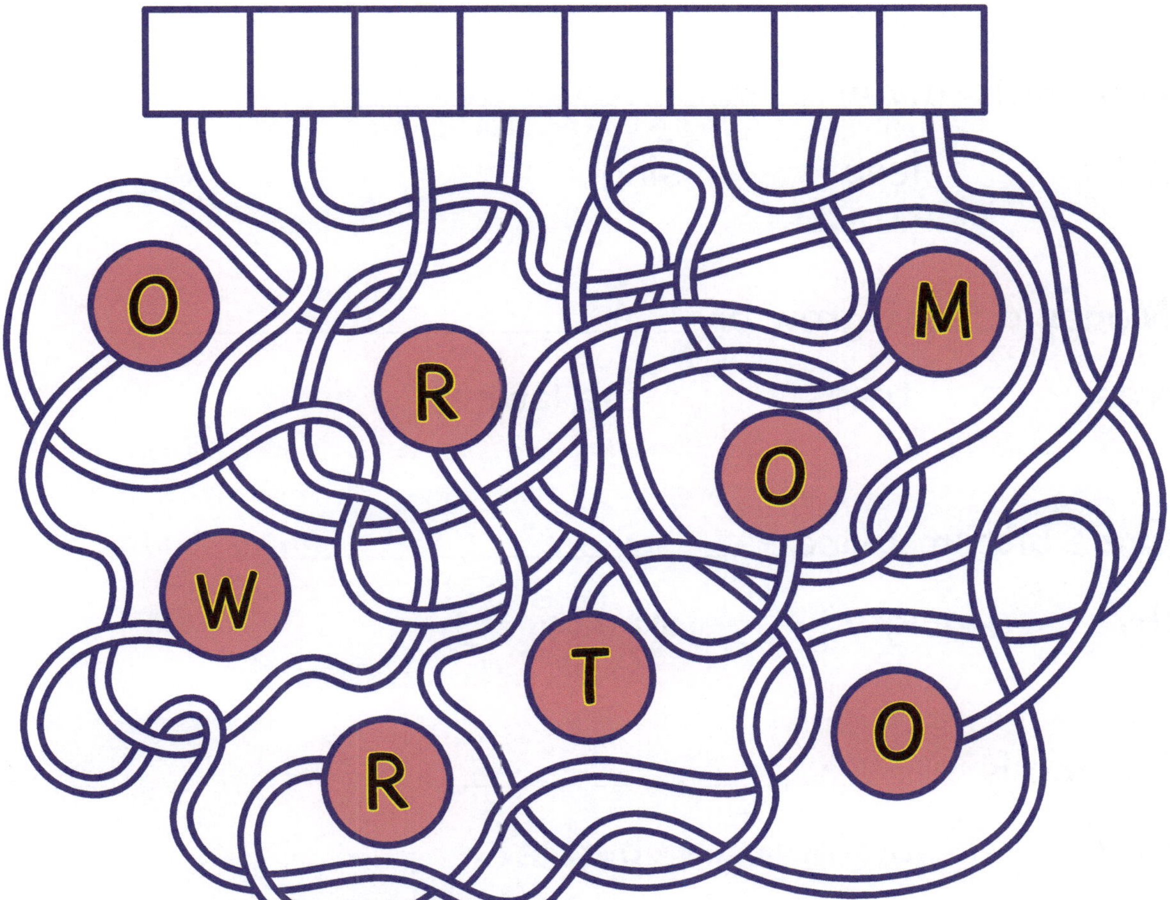

________________________ never comes.

Choose It Right

Mr Wise is trying to be extra wise and share his wisdom. Of course, he's getting it all wrong. Can you choose the right word so that his wisdom makes sense?

1. When it rains, it ______________________.

   snows hails pours

2. Look before you ______________________.

   swim leap sing

3. Money doesn't grow on ______________________.

   grass trees the lawn

4. Once bitten, twice ______________________.

   shy angry grumpy

5. Silence is ______________________.

   grey golden purple

6. The proof of the pudding is in the ______________________.

   giggling snorting eating

ANSWERS

Page 4 *The Right Choice*
1. dog 2. hand 3. fish 4. worm 5. fire

Page 5 *Crazy Crossword*
DOWN: 1. BARKING 2. CARPENTER 6. STRAW
ACROSS: 3. BAD 4. APPLE 5. GLITTERS 7. DOG
8. LEOPARD

Page 6 *Match Them Right . . .*
a rolling stone—gathers no moss; actions speak—louder than words; an eye for an eye and—a tooth for a tooth; ask no questions—and hear no lies; beggars cannot be—choosers; birds of a feather—flock together; charity begins—at home

Page 7 *Write Them Up*
1. A rolling stone gathers no moss.; 2. Actions speak louder than words.; 3. An eye for an eye and a tooth for a tooth.; 4. Ask no questions and hear no lies.; 5. Beggars cannot be choosers.; 6. Birds of a feather flock together.; 7. Charity begins at home.

Page 8 *Tick Tock*
1. bird; It is better to hold onto something one has already than to risk losing it by trying to attain something better
2. chain; An organization/a group is as strong as the laziest member.
3. friend; A person who helps at a difficult time is a person who you can really rely on.
4. penny; It is as useful to save money that you already have as it is to earn more.
5. nine; If you sort out a problem immediately it may save extra work later.

Page 9 *Juggle Muggle*
Better to do something later, rather than not do it at all.—Better late than never.; Do the things in the right order.—Don't put the cart before the horse.; Families are closer than friends.—Blood is thicker than water.; Don't be ungrateful.—Don't bite the hand that feeds you. First learn the basics. Then do the harder things.—Don't try to run before you can walk.; Don't collect your reward before you have seen the results.—Don't count your chickens before they are hatched.

Page 10 *Going Blank*
1. flies 2. horse 3. bird 4. mice 5. fleas

Page 11 *Lost Words*
1. lemonade 2. picture 3. heart 4. castle 5. candle

Page12 *Crack the Code*
HASTE MAKES WASTE

Page 13 *Egg-Stra-Ordinary*
OMELETTE

Page 14 *Picture Search*
1. bread 2. rain 3. milk 4. medicine 5. dogs 6. book

Page 16 *Crazy Crossword*
DOWN: 1. VESSELS 2. BOATS 5. SILVER 7. BED
ACROSS: 3. HORSE 4. EGGS 6. WORK 7. BRIDGE

Page 17 *The Proverb Bag*
There are two sides to every coin.—Every issue has two points of view.; The grass is always greener on the other side of the fence.—What you don't have always seems more attractive.; There's many a slip between the cup and the lip.—Many things can wrong before you get the result you want.; You can lead a horse to water, but can't make it drink.—You can't force someone to do something.

Page 18 *Decoded*
STILL WATERS RUN DEEP

Page 19 *Jumbledore*
1. love 2. nose 3. wise 4. noise 5. sun

Page 20 *Pathfinder*
Never put off until tomorrow what you can do today.

Page 21 *Tick-Tack-Toe*
1. Lightning 2. glass 3. Oil 4. father 5. head

Page 22–23 *Giddy Grid*
1. iron 2. cradle 3. smoke 4. crowd 5. evil 6. well 7. money 8. brave

Page 24 *Hard Work*
THOUSAND

Page 25 **Blank It Out**
1. house 2. Beauty 3. grass 4. boats 5. heart

Page 26 **Messy Metre**
1. broom 2. Cleanliness 3. pound 4. lunch 5. sun 6. apple

Page 28 **Crazy Crossword**
DOWN: 1. GIFT 2. SPICE 4. HOME 5. CURED
ACROSS: 2. WILL 3. SIGHT 6. ROME

Page 29 **Jumbled Up Proverbs**
1. cooks 2. cover 3. cake 4. romans 5. bridge

Page 30 **Merry Maze**
One man's meat is another man's poison.

Page 31 **Ticked Off**
1. Christmas; 2. doorstop; 3. fire; 4. mile; 5. thief

Page 32 **Match Them Right . . .**
ignorance—is bliss; it takes all sorts—to make a world; know which side—your bread is buttered; might—is right; no pain—no gain

Page 33 **And Write Them Out . . .**
1. Ignorance is bliss.; 2. It takes all sorts to make a world.; 3. Know which side your bread is buttered.; 4. Might is right.; 5. No pain, no gain.

Page 34 **Gridlocked**
1. hands 2. fall 3. shoe 4. angels 5. small

Page 35 **Proverb Maze**
Better to be poor and healthy than be happy and sick.

Page 36 **Jumble Tumble**
1. house 2. end 3. sow 4. coat 5. first

Page 37 **Hidden Words**
LINEN; GOLDEN

Page 38 **Cityscape**
1. practice 2. never 3. cheats 4. sword 5. mother 6. clothes

Page 40 **Amazing Maze**

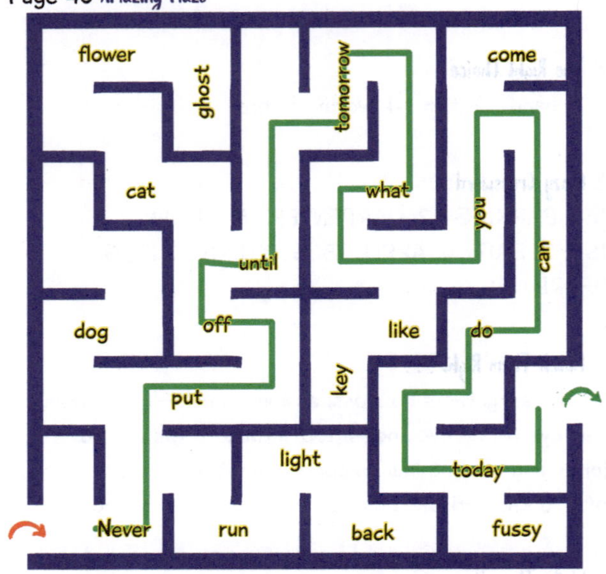

Page 41 **Mixed Up**
1. Jack of all trades, master of none. 2. Spare the rod and spoil the child. 3. Look before you leap. 4. Better pay the cook than the doctor. 5. Joy and sorrow sleep in the same bed.

Page 42 **Maze-O-Clock**
Don't ever put all your eggs in one basket.

Page 43 **Lazy Luke**
TOMORROW

Page 44 **Choose It Right**
1. pours 2. leap 3. trees 4. shy 5. golden 6. eating